A Child
Trapped Within

Amorette Hunter

A Child Trapped Within by Amorette Hunter

Copyright © 2018

ISBN-13: 978-1723546846

ISBN-10: 1723546844

Author's Disclaimer

These stories are based on true events, as imperfectly as I recall them. Names have been changed to protect the privacy of others.

Published in the Unites States of America

URIEL BOOKS
hope4hiskingdom@gmail.com

A Child Trapped Within

Amorette Hunter

URIEL BOOKS

Thank you to all those
who have supported me on my journey
reminding me that I am not alone.

Contents

1 The Hands that Hurt

Grab my throat, pin me down.

My protests mean nothing to you.

You just want to have a taste of me.

It's been in your head since the day we met.

This very moment is the one you have been waiting for. Now the time has come. You have your grip on me and you are not going to let me slither out.

Squeeze my throat until I am gasping and thrashing for a breath of air.

This is fun right? You finally have me right where you want me, underneath you because that's where a woman belongs isn't it? On the bottom? Force us down with all your might and use us up for your pleasure even against our will. Maybe if you let me take control and wait for my permission to use my body you would realize just how incredible I truly am. Nothing you can do to me will ever break me down because, you see, I am strong. I am resilient. I am not afraid of you. No matter what you think you have stolen from me, you have not. Nothing can tear my freedom away me, not even you. Not even your forceful ways.

♦   ♦   ♦

I can't breathe: he is choking me.

I try to inhale but his hands are wrapped too tight.

He is here.

I feel his hands: they travel along my body.

I smell his cologne: it tickles my nose.

I feel his hands closing around my throat.

I hear his laboured breathing: it sounds so thick and raspy.

I am back here in this place: it's like I never left.

It's all around me; the sounds, the sights, the feeling.

Everything else has drowned out and reality is gone.

It's just me.

Just him.

It's this moment over and over again. It's too real. It's too now.

♦   ♦   ♦

His hands close around forbidden parts; his mouth pressed against mine.

I squirm. I try and gasp for air but his arm is squeezing too hard around my throat and his face squished against mine. The taste of blood pours down my throat. I discreetly manage to pull on the steering wheel, making us swerve to hopefully distract him for a moment; but it doesn't affect him, as we are just rolling in an empty parking lot. I can fight this; I can get out. I can inflict pain on him to make him stop, but instead I just squirm helplessly trying to find breaks to breathe.

He grazes a finger along his face: "Why am I scratched?"

I graze my hand over a tender area: "Why am I?"

♦   ♦   ♦

Blisters on her feet.

Bruises on her knees.

Lacerations on her wrists and ankles from being bound too tight.

Trapped.

♦   ♦   ♦

Rough fingertips harshly dragging along my skin, prying at my legs and my tense body. Forcing me apart.

Frozen in fear; want to fight but paralyzed. Think about other things: the weather is supposed to be nice... I wonder what time it is.

Pain, fear, prayers.

Do you see me God? Please look away. Don't watch what is about to happen.

Shut out the world don't think.

Hyperventilating.

Just relax and breathe, you tell yourself. It will be over soon.

Shaking. Can't stop shaking.

Blackness.

A warm tear hits my leg; he feels bad. He looks at me and what he has just done with tears rolling down his face as he holds me close and tight, not wanting to lose me. He has changed: that look in his eyes is gone. His touch is strangely comforting as I lay frozen in a fetal position.

Frozen paralyzed on the floor clutching a stuffed animal with a death grip. Hoping it was a dream. Violated. This was the last straw.

He reaches out a hand and caresses my hair with a soft touch.

"I love you", he whispers over and over.

That's all that matters. He loves me.

We can get more straws.

♦   ♦   ♦

You probably think I am naive, as if I don't know what you are doing. I did not walk into this blindly. I know how it works: we play the same game over and over again. You use my body; I use you as a distraction from my emotions. You are an addict and so am I. We are trapped in the same circle and the same game. You hurt me and lower my worth with every night we have. I just make you more addicted and play with your sickness.

♦ ♦ ♦

Her insides are crying out for help but she shoves down her pain and swallows hard.

She tries to ask for help but she can never get past the small talk.

If she manages to allude to it, she quickly recovers with an 'it was nothing; I am doing great'.

She smiles bright and wide,

clutching her injured side.

'Just aches and pains', she says with a grin.

Beneath her layers lays a layer of broken flesh and bluish skin.

She rubs it like a trophy; in love with the feeling it gives,

with the downfall being that it makes her crave more pain.

A craving no one understands.

She misses the abuse, misses the danger, misses the fear, misses the injuries.

She craves the dark shades on her flesh: a scrape here and there; that look in another's eyes as they grab you with all their might so you cannot even fight. Craves that death stare. Craves the pain.

~~ The fact that you have come this far is a miracle in itself.
You survived.
You are a survivor. ~~

◆　◆　◆

I can still feel it.

I feel my body as it slams into the ground.

I feel the air in my lungs being pushed out.

I can still feel it.

I feel the fear rising up inside me.

I tense up so much that my body starts to ache.

I can still feel it.

I feel the water pouring over my motionless body.

I feel his hands rubbing me down with soap.

I can still feel it.

I feel my lungs filling up with water.

I feel his arms pushing me.

I can still feel it.

I feel the bruises left behind.

I feel my limbs being tied and crushed.

I can still hear it.

I hear the sound of my body taking each blow.

I hear my heart pounding so loud, beating through every vein.

I can still hear it.

I hear my desperate scream.

I hear my scream get silenced.

I can still see it.

I see my lifeless body on the floor.

I see him drag me across the room.

I can still see it.

I see my body on the table.
I see me getting violated.
I can still see it.

˜˜ *We are going to get through this. Together.* ˜˜

2 Comforting abuse

My body is starting to fill up with bruises; my mind is starting to fill up with anger. I grew up with this abuse. This was all I knew and it was not my choice, but now here I am choosing this life all over again. Just waiting for it to go spinning out of control as we walk around. My friends linking our arms and acting all giggly like new lovers. It's not the truth. No one knows. I don't want them to know. I don't want to leave. Abuse is where I find my comfort. I just wish this poison would leave my soul. I was gentle and kind before we met; now I feel as though I am absorbing his aggression and anger. I know how it goes. I didn't blindly stumble across this path I am now on. I read the signs from the moment we met. I felt his aggressive spirit. Yet despite everything fighting against me, I decided to go head first diving in. It's my fault. I knew better. Now I am stuck right where I wanted to be. I don't want help. I don't want out. I just want someone who will listen. Maybe this was God's dream for me.

◆　◆　◆

It happened.

It happened last night.

The tough edged fingers creeping their way prying through sealed legs and a stiff body. Hyperventilate, just breathe, relax.

Think of something else.

The weather will be nice tomorrow... Not working.

Still feel him. Still feel the pain.

Paralyzed.

Want to run want to scream. Made the decision in that moment to leave.

It is time to leave.

It's all over. Violated. Hurting. Scared.

Can't move. Gasping for air like a fish out of water.

His poison running through me.

◆ ◆ ◆

He holds me and whispers he loves me.

He loves me. It's ok.

I can't leave. I am in love with the pain.

In love with the hurt. I choose this. It is my path.

It will be ok.

˜˜*This is not love. It's time for you to go to the one true love.*˜˜

You are strong like a brick girl!

He presses his body on me.

No other option.

Maybe I should just give in. He is going to do this anyway and I won't have the strength to stop him. Maybe I should just give him what he wants.

"No!"

My voice comes out stronger than I thought it would. Louder and bolder. I was half expecting it to sound weak and shaky.

I use that as my motivation. Can't stop now. I push myself up and block myself from him.

I CAN do this.

Fight. I WILL FIGHT! I will stand up and I will win.

This is not happening anymore.

I won. I claimed the spot. This is MY body. This is MY life and this is MY choice. Respect this -- that is your only option.

Death threats don't work. Been there, done that.

"You are strong like a brick girl."

Yes. Yes, I am.

To be hurt

To be tossed to the ground till her ribs feel like they have been shattered.

To be chained so tight that chain leaves its imprint for two weeks.

So be strangled so tight that the bruises seem to stain her skin and she can hardly swallow.

To be hit so hard that an entire hand print is imprinted in her flesh.

To be held down and forced into chemicals until it eats away at her flesh and burns her skin.

To be thrown into a wall so hard that the wall breaks away.

To be beaten until she loses every bit of strength that she has.

Till she feels like a tiny ant among the earth that could just be snuffed out with a single flick of a finger.

To be stripped of any dignity she had left.

To be violated repeatedly until she is numb from the violence.

◆　◆　◆

To her it makes more sense. This, this is the way she was shown love. This is what love is. It's a language that she can understand. A language that she needs. A small price to pay. This recent endeavour calms her longing; calms the cravings. It brings her back to her home. The place where she feels the most comfort is the place where she feels the most pain.

She rubs alcohol in her fresh wounds, not as a cleaner but to feel the burn.

She deserves this pain. It makes sense. It is real. It is love.

˜˜It's false. It's a lie. You need to get out. Freedom is calling you.˜˜

Safe in the arms of the abuser

Burned.

Tattered.

Bruised.

Beaten.

Violated.

All she wants is to curl up in a ball and get surrounded with an embrace.

She cuddles up to the one who laid his hand on her.

The only one who she can lean in to is the one who leave the bruises.

Is the one who violates.

She feels so ashamed and so violated.

She has fresh wounds covering her body.

She just needs someone to hold her.

He wraps her up tight in his arms.

Her knees are tight to her chest and her breathing is rapid.

She feels so young.

She just needs someone to comfort her.

Someone to hold her tight in a safe and warm embrace.

He holds her close and rubs her back.

His hand passes across the fresh marks he made.

He is the only one who comforts her.

The one who abuses her.

The one who uses her.

The one who leaves the marks.

Holds her close tonight.

◆   ◆   ◆

Laying still she pretends to sleep.

Maybe he will stop if she is asleep.

She tries to adjust her breaths to a more sleep-like breathing pattern.

His hands grab tightly at her legs pulling her in close to his warm body.

She lays limp as a rag doll still pretending to be asleep.

His hands digging in so hard that pain shoots in through her legs.

She cannot take it anymore.

She tries to toss: he grabs her even tighter until she lets out a yelp of pain.

She tries to wriggle out of his grasp and squirm away, but her mind is so clouded from the drugs that she has hardly any strength left to escape.

She manages to escape his hold for long enough that she could roll onto her back and fight him off with her legs.

Struggling on the bed they fight with each other until he manages to get a good hold on her.

Lifting her up he throws her off of the bed (she is just a child so he can do this with ease as he throws her small frame into the air).

She hits the ground with a force strong enough to break ribs and the air is forced out of her lungs: she lets out a yelp and he lands on her body crushing her small body underneath of his large frame.

She wriggles and fights with everything she has - ignoring the pain she feels - but his sheer size and mass outdoes hers by miles.

He yells at her to stop fighting but she refuses to give up: she will not stop.

She will not give in.

He manages to grab her arms and tie them together: they are so tight her fingers start to swell up and turn purple.

She still fights.

She still tries to get him off.

He gets increasingly frustrated: with his knee full force into her back, he wraps his hands around her throat and he squeezes tight while she continues to fight underneath him.

The air in her lungs trapped; her hands tied; the spots begin to cloud her vision - she can feel the life being drained out of her - she does not want to give up fighting him off.

"This is it", she thinks. "It's finally happening." In a bittersweet moment, she thinks, "I will finally be free from these chains."

Her body has no strength left; no fight left, and all her limbs fall loose and limp.

˜˜*You have got to leave.*

You have got to go before it is too late˜˜

3 ED

Why is it so hard? Just pick up a fork and eat something. It sounds so simple, your stomach aches and it grumbles begging and pleading for something - for anything - and yet you deny your body of the one thing it needs the most. The smell of food becomes nauseating. Invites to dinner are stressful. Everything revolves around food: all gatherings normally include people hovering over some sort of food. Someone always complains that they ate too much. "Oh, I shouldn't eat this", they say as they fill their face with more. When food becomes your enemy you turn down invites with your friends to meal events, secluding yourself just a little bit more, so you are alone in your battle.

◆ ◆ ◆

It's all consuming.

A poison that runs through her body.

Does she even go a moment without focusing on her body?

It seems like a constant thought.

She runs until her legs collapse underneath her.

Sleep seems to be a thing of the past, replaced by counting steps and finding calorie burning methods.

35,398 steps.

473 calories consumed.

1.4 lbs a day, dropped.

Numbers rolling through her head over and over.

The obsession is taking over everything.

◆ ◆ ◆

Recovered

The numbers are on the rise.

It drives you so crazy you could scream but you keep eating.

"Wow you are doing so good: I am so proud of you."

If only you really knew.

Smile. Just smile and say thank you.

Eat a little more; make sure they see you because it's healthy, right?

You're supposed to. Maybe ask for seconds, you probably should even Instagram it so the whole world knows how healthy you are: Oh look at me, I really do eat.

Your leg starts bouncing. Maybe it will bounce the calories right off.

"Wow, you are just glowing."

Yeah, you know what else glows?

My blade as I slice my skin open because I disgust myself so much.

No, don't say that.

Smile and nod.

"I am so glad you are better!"

AM I???? IS THIS BETTER????

I hate my body so much, I am in physical pain and feel like throwing myself in front of a train!

Maybe don't say that either.

Smile and with as much enthusiasm as you can muster say, "Thank you. It has been a journey but I made it!"

But you haven't made it, have you?

No. Your body may not be, but you are dying. From the inside out from an illness that no one will ever see or ever understand.

You beg for it to end.

The torture gets too much.

But hey, your skin is glowing and you have a bit of extra fat hugging your waist, so you're not dying, right? You are recovered

All better. Just like that! Ta da!

Yeah... right...

˜˜Try and have just a little. One small bite.
    Feel the texture in your mouth; let the flavour awaken you. ˜˜

◆ ◆ ◆

Bones

Ribs and hips.

Collar bones and shoulder bones.

Pinch, pull, measure, slice, repeat.

Dizzy, nauseous, light headed, cold.

Run, jog, walk.

Snap, crackle, pop go the joints.

Joint ache, stomach ache, head ache, feet ache, everything ache.

Alcohol, pills, laxatives, caffeine.

Puke buckets, blades, scales, measuring tapes.

Exhausted, hair loss, chipping nails, irritable.

Bones.

Cheek bones, knees, wrists, jaw line.

Pinch, pull, measure, slice, repeat.

All consuming sickness.

◆ ◆ ◆

She hates the sight of herself every mirror she passes stares at her like an enemy warping her vision.

Her hip bones stick out so far it hurts to lay down.

Counting her calories: trying to stay under 100 daily.

She no longer feels hunger. Her body has grown used to its intake amount.

Stepping on the scale, she yells out in frustration as the number seems to go up instead of down.

Running laps around the kitchen island after eating a throat lozenge, trying to burn off the excess calories.

Restless at night for the fear that weight gain will happen while she sleeps, she does as many crunches as she possibly can.

Her clothes don't fit like they used to; too loose around the waist, causing such a frustration. A madness that makes her rip all her clothes out of the closet and throw them onto the floor. Nothing fits: too loose and yet still too fat in them. Maybe there is a way to tear off your skin. She grabs a knife and presses it hard into her stomach. It doesn't pierce the skin.

She throws the knife onto the ground. MAKE IT STOP.

MAKE IT STOP!

She swears repeatedly at the top of her lungs, putting on her music full blast trying to drown out her thoughts.

♦ ♦ ♦

Wrapped up tight in the fetal position Rocking back and forth, your insides are screaming.

Everything in you is screaming.

You dig your nails so hard into your side they cut through your flesh and it burns.

You need to slice your skin.

You need to punish yourself

You ate too much.

You didn't exercise enough.

You let people come close to you.

You don't deserve love.

You need to be punished.

You need to be set back.

You're not allowed to move forward.

You tried to break out of your chains, step out of your bubble but you're not allowed.

Go back into your cage: it's where you belong.

You are not free.

You are a puppet.

My puppet.

~~DO NOT listen to the lies; they seek to destroy you. You HAVE to overcome this.~~

♦ ♦ ♦

So dizzy she falters in her steps.

A nausea that seems to never leave.

Her bones crack and ache as she steps.

676 calories consumed today.

1 lb lost, more to go.

Finally back on track.

Finally feeling in control.

Everything feels so much better now.

Push down all the other feelings.

Let this distraction take over.

♦ ♦ ♦

I cannot stop shivering, shaking so bad my teeth chatter and everyone stops to offer me a jacket or ask if I am okay.

The numbers are going up; I cannot sit down until they go down.

You lose more calories standing up.

At least I burn calories while I shiver.

So nauseated I feel like vomiting. The smell of food drives me insane. I am starving.

Drink water to fill up my stomach and to clean out my body.

Hungry? Drink a litre of water.

˜˜I wish you could see yourself as I see you.
  You are so beautiful. ˜˜

♦   ♦   ♦

I can't help but run my fingers along my back, pinching the fat in between my fingers and tugging it.

Maybe I could just cut it off with scissors.

Trace along my collar bones, measuring how deep they sink in.

The panic starts to hit when I look in the mirror. I can see and feel the squishy bits that lay over my bones.

Looking in the mirror. A close-up of my face.

Dark circles under my eyes.

Wrinkles that run so deep they leave permanent lines on my face.

How did I get here? I can't stand the person staring back at me.

Another year older, it's terrifying. It's a haunting reminder of who I have become.

I keep thinking in my head of all the ways I could just end this.

Put a stop to it all. The numbers would end and stop going up. The scale, the timeline: it would all be over.

Finished. Freedom.

The scale has become such a daunting thing, it haunts me when I stand on it and see the numbers rise. I jump off it quickly before the numbers can fully calculate.

It's hard to sleep at night. I toss and turn; maybe the more I toss, the more calories I will burn. All I can think of is the weight on my body and how my skin is not what it used to be.

I feel like screaming but instead I curl up on my side in a tight ball, vibrating and digging my nails into my flesh; wishing I could just claw my way out of this body. I glance at the clock and the minutes turn into hours. It's a night that never ends. I try and focus on something different but my thoughts automatically go back into self-hatred.

I grab my pillow and squeeze it so hard a bit of stuffing squishes out the seam. Like my fat as it squishes out my ripped jeans when I sit down. The roll that piles over my waist line on my pants. The doctor says I can't lose any more weight I am becoming dangerously underweight. He pulls out the death card: you are going to die if you keep going like this. Why don't you see what I do??? Are you blind? Don't you see the rolls of fat? My legs are so thick, I have a muffin top. This is far from too thin.

I have to lose more.

I NEED TO LOSE IT ALL.

I am stuck in a skin and a body that is not mine.

4 Red light

Her slender legs clatter together. Fear shoots down her small frail frame. Salty tears run down her face, into the crevice of her button nose. Down her cracked pink lips and her bruised chin.

Tilting her head down, she watches the salty tear fall to a cold cement floor; a floor that holds thousands of salty tears. She knows this is her destiny. This is what she was meant to do. Wiping her face with the back of her blood-speckled hand, she attempts to stand tall.

She gazes up at the men in front of her, arguing and exchanging money. She is just a child.

◆　◆　◆

Put on your sexy heels.

Hike up your skirt.

Show them what sin is.

They won't mind the bruises or the fresh track marks along your veins.

Snakes flowing through your blood.

A smile that doesn't reach beyond your mouth.

A forced giggle that escapes your mouth so easily it shocks you

They won't mind...

~**Lips**.

◆　◆　◆

She walks in the middle of the road.

A car honks from behind her yet she does not move to the side.

She outstretches her arms as if to say "hit me".

She places a foot along the yellow line and walks along it as though it is a tightrope.

Balancing for her life.

The car gives up on honking and accelerates around her, spinning its tires as it goes.

Oh, please just hit me, she begs a silent plea.

Reaching out to people over text, yet it seems as though they go unanswered: all but one.

All but that one person. He always replies within moments: there at the drop of a hat.

However with everything there comes a price.

A price you must pay for this type of arrangement. She just needs out of her head. He provides her that way out for a small fee.

A price she is more than willing to pay.

Coming down the road she sees his vehicle up ahead. A way out of her mind; a way out of her memories; a way out of theses emotions and these feelings.

He lets out a little honk and pulls off to the side of the road so she can hop in.

No matter the time, he is always there. A poison, yet a medicine.

The price is small enough.

◆ ◆ ◆

I don't know what to do anymore. I burn bridges I fight people who are trying to help and I am stubborn. I am sick of this. I am sick of life, sick of myself. Maybe I will actually get murdered this time. Maybe this will be my last and final trick.

I can't do this anymore. I am sick of fighting and I am sick of "god" ignoring my cries as I fall back down to the ground and he shoves my face into the dirt.

I am done.

◆ ◆ ◆

I have been robbed.
Why did I do this for free.
You can play so long as you pay.
But you didn't .
You grabbed me.
You flipped me over.
You violated me.
And that's okay.
So long as you pay.
But you didn't.
You treat me as your toy, your rag doll.
I don't mind but you must participate in the exchange.
You take, you give.
But you didn't.
Is that rape?
I didn't want it.
I guess I just let you.
My no wasn't loud enough.
Violated.
Robbed.
Used.
Abused.
At least it gives me something interesting to write about.

◆ ◆ ◆

Red dress.
Red light.
Just a mess.

Just a night.

~Lips.

♦   ♦   ♦

His hands travel up your legs.

He starts at your toes; they curl in response to his touch.

Not because they like it but because they dread it.

Almost like they are trying to hide.

Your muscles tense as his hands travel up further and further.

"Oh please not tonight," you think to yourself.

You can't fight him off; you can't tell him no.

You can just pray he will stop.

That it won't get that far tonight.

However, this is the price.

This is your job.

So you swallow your pride and any dignity that you have left and you take it.

You need to put food on the table somehow.

Bills don't pay themselves.

The sound of his breathing changes.

His breath is revolting; his body odor is so strong it almost masks the smell of cat litter and urine that has become his only cologne.

"Why?" you ask yourself as you feel his heavy body land against yours: "Why do I always do this?"

It's a question that so many have asked you, and a question you ask yourself as well.

Is it the money? Is it the lifestyle?

You are constantly disgusted with yourself and hating your decisions and yet you continue to make them.

He moans repulsively, interrupting your thoughts.

His breathing sounds more like snoring.

There is nothing about this to enjoy: the sound of his flabby body slapping away.

His disgusting flesh seems to engulf your body as you lay there and wish that you didn't have to do this.

 ~~~ *If I can use my story to save even just one life,*
       it will all be worth it. ~~~

♦   ♦   ♦

Friday night.

In the same place all over again.

Feeling guilty.

I shouldn't be here

A pain burns through my chest.

I shouldn't be here.

Guilt rushes through me like a river breaking through rocks.

I shouldn't be here.

Hands tighten around my neck.

I shouldn't be here.

I see spots.

My oxygen is leaving.

I shouldn't be here.

Everything starts going black.

Darkness.

Suffocating.

I shouldn't have been there.

Just another bad trick.

˜˜This is not some glittered glorified life. You don't want this.˜˜

♦   ♦   ♦

I don't know why I'm here. I'm back again.
I've left so many times saying I need to stay away: all I see is violence.
all I see is hurt.
all I see is lies.
all I see is pain.
These streets just keep pulling me back.

♦   ♦   ♦

Rain drops.
Tear stains.
Drops like ice slicing her skin.
Cold to the bones.
Hair standing as tall as it can along her bare legs.
Air fogging as she slightly exhales.
Whiskey sliding down.
Burning her throat.
Sweet sensation.
~Lips.

♦   ♦   ♦

Her worlds are starting to collide.
She is forgetting who she is.
Maybe this is who she was the whole time.
Maybe she is now pulling down the mask and revealing the truth.
Her friends see and they become part of her game
No longer friends now they want what she has to offer.

A little bit of her body to go around for all.

~Lips.

♦   ♦   ♦

She is forced to sell her body, a slave to a man.

When she looks in the mirror all she sees is a price tag, a beaten and used piece of meat.

She can't leave. If she leaves he will find her, and he will bring harm to her friends.

So she remains, as men use her.

Repeatedly.

Day after day.

Night after night.

Day-dreaming of freedom.

~~I see you. You are not alone.~~

♦   ♦   ♦

The air is brisk the smell of alcohol is so thick it tingles your tongue. A breeze rolls through the air. It carries the sound of distant sirens and arguing voices.

A scream pierces through the air. It sends chills down your spine. Chills that run through your arms and down to your fingertips.

It's an average night.

Screams.

Fights.

Sirens.

Your fingers clatter together in the night. Your nails are chipping off. Your bones are sore and weak.

Your body seems to be screaming at you to stop.

Stop the pain.

Stop the abuse.

But you can't. This is what you were born to do.

It's your job.

You walk the streets, flash a smile and grab some quick cash. The streets are the only thing you know. You own them.

Ignoring the chill in the air, your lips that are turning blue, you lift up your dress a little higher. Your joints burn as the cold air goes rushing to your knees.

Pain is what you live for.

Pain is what you'll die for.

~Lips.

˜˜ *The night is too cold. Stay inside tonight.* ˜˜

♦   ♦   ♦

Needle in my vein.

Bit of cash in my hand.

~Lips.

♦   ♦   ♦

Maybe it's the anxiety.

Maybe it's the addiction.

Maybe it's the money.

Selling my soul.

Selling my body.

It's the only thing I know how to do.

Hurt me, abuse me, step on me.

It's the only love I know.

Have clients take me to church after the deed is done.

Sit in the service side by side, both worshipping the same god.

Repent.

Do it all over again after the service.

"Thanks for the lift, here's your payment."

Use me, abuse me, hurt me.

It's all I know.

I am not a victim.

Just chained to a dark path that won't let me go.

˜˜You are valuable. You are worth far more than any price tag.˜˜

♦　♦　♦

She knows how to move.

She's so smooth.

She's like a black panther.

She slinks in with her irresistible movements.

A snarl from her mouth.

A lick of her lips.

Will have you begging for more.

Once she sinks her teeth into you leaving her mark you will be forever addicted.

She will be the goddess of your dreams.

You will follow her around to the end of the earth just to have another taste of her velvet body.

The way her hips sway.

In such an irresistible way.

She comes at a price.

Those heels don't come for free.

Pay her nice .

She's sure to entice.

Treat her right.

Because she does bite.

When she has cleaned out your wallet.

You have to say goodbye.

You can have her body as your own, if the price is right.

Don't think she will think about you twice when you are gone.

She's a tigress on the prowl .

Looking for her next prey.

Bleed them dry and move on.

She spends her riches on the naughtiest of things.

She will put it stashed away for a later date.

She will have you begging.

Begging for more.

~Lips.

♦   ♦   ♦

Pupils dilated.

Words slurred.

Body moving to the beat.

Strobe lights flashing.

Ear drums bursting.

Selling love.

♦   ♦   ♦

Let her out to play.

She stays inside locked away.

Waiting for her moment to pounce.

She just wants a little fun.

Prowling in her cage she paces back and forth.

She growls low and deep.

Like a thunder that will shake your house and keep you awake.

She is completely harmless to you.

Just let her out and you will see.

She will give you the riches of the world if you just let her play.

Let her do her thing.

She works better at night in the cover of the dark, but if you let her out in the day that will also be okay.

She will do what she was born to do.

Seduce.

She will get your bills paid, she sees you struggling to make ends meet. Just trust her to do her thing.

She will bring you no harm. After all, you are her, and she is you.

Just let me out .

Let me put to play.

~Lips.

˜˜There is no price tag high enough to sell your soul.˜˜

♦   ♦   ♦

In the moment of transaction, she wonders if it's worth it. She wonders if she could just leave and change her ways.

Be free forever and live a different life. Make a new story.

She just wants it to be over and wants to be done.

Trying to do everything she can to not think about what is happening, she daydreams and lets her mind wander away to a different place.

A place where she is happy. A place where her life is one that she likes and enjoys

♦   ♦   ♦

Slab of meat.

She has been through so many hands.

Passed around more than the money she holds.

Her heels click away on the floor as she struts her stuff.

Men's hands fondle her body as she swings on the pole.

They surround her and circle her like sharks all licking their lips and trying to have a taste.

Grabbing her wrists to try to pull her in if they get the chance.

She easily and flirtatiously shakes them off and wriggles out of their grasps dipping herself back holding onto the pole with only a leg.

Everyone is in line to buy her.

They all want to pay for a taste of body.

So many have used her.

So many have abused her.

So many hands have held her.

So many have tried to claim her.

Under those flashing lights she moves her body in sync with the beat.

She has forgotten who she is in the heat of it all and forgets she is human at all.

She is just a toy for their pleasure.

A puppet in the night. Oh...

She is just a slab of meat.

5 ADDICT

It runs through her veins.
Killing her pains.
Entering her mind.
Never knowing what it'll find.
Erasing all the memories.
That seem to go back centuries.
It is just a temporary erase.
As it wraps her in its embrace.
And now she's free.
Can't you see.
Living in a false reality.
That could lead to fatality.
All you can do now is pray.
That she is okay.
Life is such a blur.
No one wants to deal with her .
No one can hear her cries.
They just say their goodbyes.
They all walk away.
Leaving her till another day.
A day when she's in a good space.
And not such a nutcase.
Leaving her to fight alone.
Getting closer to her tombstone.
But that's okay.

He hears her pray.
Every day in the same way.
"I'll get high.
Take me to the sky.
Just let me die."

♦   ♦   ♦

I know it's late and I should get to sleep. I have reached the bottom of the bottle, where to go now?
Lost .

˜˜*Call your sponsor.*˜˜

♦   ♦   ♦

Feel it rush through your veins.
It clouds your head.
It clouds your mind.
It's hard to tell what reality even is.
The world spins around and around.
It brings you a sense of happiness.
Even if just for a moment you get to escape reality and find something a little nicer.
Set aside your thoughts and worries.
Let it take over you like a wave.
Engulfing you into its dream world.

˜˜*Reach out*˜˜

♦   ♦   ♦

Shivering, shaking, tickles down your spine.

A stupid grin that won't leave your face.

Oh what a beautiful taste.

Oh that artificial happiness.

A giggle that is too loud.

A mind that is seeing things that are not even there.

◆　◆　◆

"You are not alone, you are not alone."

The words swirled through her mind as she anxiously awaited a reply from somebody, anybody.

Not a word.

Her face flushed, her hands balled up in tight little fists, her breathing rapid, her heart racing. She needed her fix. Needed her relief.

She cried out for someone, no one came.

Brushed off.

Alone.

In the dark.

She needed her fix.

◆　◆　◆

Fists relaxing, heart slowing, sigh of relief, drop of blood trickling along her arm.

Just a little fix.

Not nearly enough but enough for the craving to be temporally caged.

˜˜*No matter how much you shoot into your veins,*
   the memories will never leave. ˜˜

◆　◆　◆

Feel it rushing through you.

It sloshes through your veins like a water slide.

It pools into your heart making it beat a little faster at the impact.

It fills into every crevice of your body.

When it reaches your fingers they start to rumble and tremble to an unheard beat.

It runs along your arms making your hair stand up and tingle.

It gets to your eyes and it plays its magic tricks making your pupils dilate.

And flashes of images appear that no one else can see.

It enfolds your brain and dances along, rearranging your thoughts and distorting your thought patterns.

Just long enough for you to forget for a moment.

6 THE INSIDES

"WHO ARE YOU???" you scream at the top of your lungs.

You have been screaming for so long your throat burns.

Your face is beet-red and hot. You can feel your heart beating inside your throat.

You look at the person who stares back at you and you feel such a hatred you just want to punch in their teeth: everything about them is so disgusting. The way their teeth are yellowed, the way their hair sits in a hideous mess. All you can think about is wrapping your hands around their throat and holding until they can no longer breathe.

"WHO ARE YOU???" you continue to yell at them.

When you look at them you see how worthless they are. Oh, how pitifully they stare back at you as you yell at them.

You hate everything about them. You hate the things they wear, the way they talk, the way they move, the way they smell.

You don't even know who they are.

All you know is that it you cannot stand them.

You have no idea who is even staring back at you.

Just another fight with the mirror.

♦ ♦ ♦

I don't want to be alone tonight. The darkness is seeping in. It hurts.

I sit on the floor in a little ball and hug my knees close to my chest in hopes to bring myself comfort. Make it stop. The memories; they hurt. I am okay. I am okay. I repeat it over and over in my head but I am not. No I am not. It hurts so much my insides are screaming. Oh God, please save me from this pain. It hurts so much I can hardly breathe.

Please hold me close. Wrap your arms around me and hold me. Don't let go. Please make this go away. I cannot take this anymore. I can't fight off these feelings. I can't fight off these memories. Please help me. I don't want to be alone.

◆   ◆   ◆

You are on the edge of a break down.

Your head starts feeling hot .

You feel your heart pounding.

All you want is to scream.

Scream.

Scream.

Scream.

But there are no sounds that come out.

You frantically try and put music on as loud as you can to drown yourself out .

Drown out your thoughts.

Drown out the images.

Drown out yourself.

Your laptop freezes and refuses to play music.

The images start rolling faster through your head.

Your lungs seem to twist themselves tight, so your breathing is fast and laboured.

Gasping for more air.

Your stomach starts rolling around and you feel like you are about to puke.

Falling to the floor you clench your fists so hard your nails feel like they are going to pierce your skin.

You rock yourself back and forth on the floor waiting for it to end.

Waiting for the feelings to leave.

Waiting for the images to leave.

Waiting.

Waiting.

◆　◆　◆

When the sun goes down and the darkness blankets the streets, my mind wanders back. Back to the times I was a little child. I think to myself: that is what I deserve. To sleep on the streets. To shiver in a playground, curled up under a slide trying to stay warm, as the winter air swirls around my toes, making them so cold I can hardly stand.

"That is what you deserve", slurs the snake. "That is what you were born for". Oh, how I wish I could be back in the time when I was drinking out of a brown paper bag curled up beside that brick wall. I can still feel the texture of the wall beneath my fingertips. It is rough and prickly. It is edged you see; it's not a smooth wall. It's a wall I have walked into after too many drinks from that paper bag. After too many hits from that needle.

Life seemed almost simpler then in some warped way.

Under the blanket of night I got what I deserved, as I was forced against that wall. Shoved so hard it made me bleed. Dropping my bottle in the paper. It fell to the ground and shattered. That warm whiskey spilled out on the streets like the blood of the girls there before me.

"This is where you belong," slithered the snake as the man forced himself inside me. "This is all you will ever be. Nothing more just a piece of garbage on the side of the street. Oh, how sweet is the sound of your pain and the tears that roll down your cheeks."

This is where I am meant to be. Going 240 down the highway in the passenger seat as he grips my arm and shoves me hard. I cling on trying not to fall out. I can already see it in my mind as my body meets the pavement and I say my goodbyes.

This is where I belong. I am his prisoner. He has chained me up from head to feet. The details are fuzzy. "Oh dear God, is this the night we meet?"

This is where I belong. A slave of the night forced like a puppet to pull these tricks.

Like a dog chained up for life, I pull on my chains. They rattle against the ground and against the posts. I pull so hard on my neck that it chokes me and I can't breathe. Trapped in the basement. No one can hear me but myself. The tug on the chains seem to bring me a false comfort. "This is your home now. This is what you are supposed to be," sneers the snake.

This is where I belong this man is on top of me forcing me down he has ripped away every bit of fight and strength I have and is now using me up like so many other have.

This is where I belong: a small child locked in a garage with a man who only wants to play games with a small little girl who has not even developed. I try to get away but he crunches on my frail wrists. I am careful not to shout out, for what lays beyond the garage is a far worse fate than what he will do to me. So I just accept this.

This is where I belong. A child trapped, a child abused.

This is what I deserve. A slave to drugs. A slave to the bottle that reaches the bottom all too quickly.

"Just shoot up a little more, my little girl, and you will find yourself in a better place."

I try to take it all away. I shoot up so much that it should be the end.

I down bottle after bottle of all the pills. If I puke I shove them down again.

I mix drugs with alcohol trying to find the best suicide mix. See, I don't want a quick death. I want it to be so long and painful that I will be screaming out, because that is what I deserve. I want every ounce of my body to be in pain, burning from head to toe.

I try to jump off a bridge, plunging into deep waters. I can't swim. You see, surely I will drown and my lungs will fill up with water as I try to scream for air.

However, it seems like the snake pulls me out and says "Good try, but you will never be free from me because this life is your hell."

I gasp for air on the side of the bank screaming, "Please kill me, God. If you are out there, take my life away".

The snake just laughs and laughs as he sees my despair.

This is what I deserve.

This is where I am meant to be. Laying behind a dumpster covered in my own filth and blood, naked and cold.

"Next time, kill me" I mutter as I stumble away.

Maybe my next trick will be my last. Maybe he will kill me. Please just set me free.

This is where I deserve to be. There are so many men hovering over me. My mind is so clouded. I know I have been drugged. I reach for my phone and text out a plea.

"Please help me.

I think I have been drugged."

I wander off from where they dumped me and hobble my way outside a police station. I can't see anything. I can hardly move. I lay down on the ground and try to knock on the door. I can feel the glass under my hand. My thick ring makes a clunking sound that seems to bring comfort. I hear a voice say my name, but I still keep knocking.

Maybe this is it. Maybe this door is Hell's gates. Just let me in.

I am done being here. I just keep knocking. I hear voices in the background. "Yeah I know her; she is a regular."

A regular here at Hell's gates. Here I am face down in the snow. Just let me into these gates of hell. I feel myself being dragged away from the gates. People are poking and prodding me. I can't see. My vision is so blurry.

I hear the words, "ignore her she is probably fine".

How can it be? This is what I deserve. A world of shame. Even in my darkest most vulnerable moments, as I cry out for help, I get shunned like a stray dog begging for food.

This is what I deserve: the shame, the memories, are my torture.

This is what I deserve: the tournament every night that keeps me lying awake, that flows through my dreams, the horrors that I relive every single day. I deserve these memories and so much more.

Every night as the sun goes down and his darkness covers the ground like a thick heavy blanket I yell it: "God take back the night, that snake has stolen too many".

♦ ♦ ♦

The sounds in the night make her wince.

She curls up tight.

Shielding her head.

Peering over her knees every once in a while.

She rocks back and forth ever so slightly.

She flinches and suppresses a screech every time the floors creak or the neighbours make a peep.

Her heart beats so fast she overheats.

Terrified of touch.

Terrified of people.

Terrified of sounds.

Maybe if someone could just grab her and hold her while she recedes into a smaller tighter ball and shakes in fear.

Maybe, just maybe, she might start to relax.

It won't be easy; she might fight.

She might scream with fright.

But maybe, just maybe, a father could hold her tight.

Letting her know she will be alright.

Maybe then she could find rest.

◆ ◆ ◆

She is flying high tonight.

Her eyes glisten like dew on grass.

It's the only time she feels alive.

She is hardly human at all.

The life she lives is what your nightmares are made of.

The things she desires, the things she craves, are the things you would never wish upon your worst enemy.

The pain she craves.

She feels the most comfortable while she is being tortured.

It's what she knows best; it's all that she wants.

◆ ◆ ◆

I just want to be free.

◆ ◆ ◆

I hear it all the time.

"It's a miracle you're alive."

But sometimes I wish.

It wasn't like this.

My smile never touches my eyes.

Everywhere I look are chains and walls.

Bars and bricks.

"Tear them down in Jesus' name."

They shout it out.

I raise my arms in praise, agreeing with the Lord.

It's time to be free.

Enough of this.

And maybe for a moment the walls seem to disappear, I am finally free.

I praise the God who sets the captives free.

I surrender it all, just me and my King.

But as the songs end, and the speaker comes "Thank you all for coming today," it all comes rushing back.

The walls are built back up, the chains bind me again, reality hits me like a truck, taking away my breath.

I am stuck drowning in a tank.

Reaching out and trying to grasp onto something to pull myself out. Yet in all my efforts I just sink more.

I sink.

I sink.

I sink.

Down into the darkness.

"Welcome back," the enemy sneers, gripping me tight.

The freedom was nice while it lasted.

◆   ◆   ◆

They tell me "It's a miracle you have survived."

I may be alive, but I am not living.

I may smile yet it's only on the surface.

These thoughts swarm around me dragging me down further.

My body may be here.

But I am six feet under.

˜˜Don't let go.˜˜

♦   ♦   ♦

I can't be fixed. I am trapped.

I guess I'll admit it:

I am in pain.

So much pain that there seems to be only one way to end it.

I won't do that. Not tonight, anyway. No, tonight I fight like every night before. Every night, every day, every moment a battle.

My life a battlefield.

So much blood.

So much death. So much pain surrounding me.

But hey, that's just reality.

Constantly plagued by the thought of mortality.

♦   ♦   ♦

Peel back my skin, layer by layer.

I'm a caged animal trapped by my own skin.

Let me out.

Set me free.

Can't take the torment.

Can't take the pain.

Let me out.

Set me free.

Trapped inside of a body that's not mine.

I'm screaming. Can you hear me?

I'm screaming on the inside.

Let me out.

Set me free.

Can't take the torment.

Can't take the pain.

~~*Lift up your head now, child. Don't look so sad. I have got you. I am holding you close tonight. You will be safe. The morning will come and the sun will be out again.*~~

◆   ◆   ◆

You have not even yet closed your eyes, yet you realize that you are breathing as though you just completed a marathon.

"And it begins," you grumble to yourself.

Afraid to sleep for a fear of the things you will see.

The trauma, the tournament, the abuse;

It's as though it's happening all over again.

Every night you sleep,

You get raped,

You get beat,

You get tormented,

All over again.

You wake up exhausted as though you never slept at all.

As your eyes fall heavy, the images start to flash. You fight yourself to stay awake;

To convince yourself it's just a dream.

Yet you can only stay awake for so long until your body takes over and forces you to sleep.

Fading away, it all comes back again.

It's happening all over again.

Just wake up.

You can never escape this nightmare.

You thought you were free, yet every time you close your eyes you are reminded that you are not.

You are forever trapped in a memory.

◆   ◆   ◆

She slaps on a smile and talks away.

Half the time she has no idea what she is saying.

She talks to fill the silence.

It's silence that kills her.

Silence that lets her brain think.

Silence that brings back memories of pain.

Flashes of memories that she denies.

"Oh sorry, I blanked out,"

She says with a rather convincing grin.

She swallows hard and reminds herself: there are so many people out there in real pain.

It's ok. I can handle this.

She continues to talk and let the words pour out of her mouth like a river.

She gets out and runs quickly to a source of music to shut off her brain.

She is not in pain; she is fine.

She puts on her tough face and lies her way through another day. A smile here, a laugh there. No one really knows what's beneath that. No one really sees past her laughs and smiles.

No one sees what she actually thinks and what she feels:

The pain inside her that is destroying her.

She masked herself so well that she can't take it off.

˜˜*You are not done yet. This is just the beginning. Don't you want to hold on and see your story till the very end? Don't cut it short.*˜˜

◆　◆　◆

Looking in the mirror she wants to peel off her skin.

This isn't her face.

This isn't her body.

She stares blankly at the person who stares blankly back at her.

She glances at her hands and her arms absorbing the details she catches.

Her skin is etched with silvery white lines: some straight, some crooked, some in a neat little row, and some just so randomly put, they look quite out of place.

Creases here, dry skin there.

Little red dot crawling along a vein.

Just a reminder of some other pain.

This isn't her time; this isn't her place.

She wants to scream.

She wants to go back.

This isn't her body, this isn't her face

◆　◆　◆

I don't even know what I am feeling all I know is my mind can't take it.

I just need release. Slice me open and bleed me dry. Drain it all out till I die.

Dig a hole and bury me alive. Let the dirt fill my lungs as I choke and sputter my last breath. Let the darkness engulf me.

Smash me into a wall.

Let me fall.

Let my knees hit the ground so hard they break and shatter.

Let me feel the pain.

I swear I am going insane.

I am on the edge and I am falling.

Hanging on for dear life. Fighting against an unseen force that pushes me down so hard and drives me to the edge.

I slip a bit and lose my footing.

Falling.

Falling.

Falling.

Can anyone hear my pleas for help?

They are so quiet. I don't want to disturb people.

I am embarrassed to ask for help because here I am again. I know you are sick of it. I feel so terrible for you.

At first you worry, but then it gets old.

You say "oh, here we go again".

As I dangle off the edge for the thousandth time, fighting off an invisible force that no one can see.

To you it looks like I am just fooling around dancing carelessly at the edge again and putting myself there on purpose.

You don't feel the blows from the force as they hit me so hard.

You don't see me as I try and fight back with everything I have in me.

To you I am just messing around.

You don't feel as the life is being pulled out of me.

I don't want to ask for help. I relentlessly try to pull myself back up on my own as I have done all my life. I fight and struggle. My small little arms just never seem to be strong enough.

I want to scream. I want to yell. I want to fight this off but no sounds escape me.

I am falling.

Maybe this will be the time.

Maybe this will be the time I can't pull myself up.

Maybe this will be the time I lose this battle.

Maybe this time I fall.

Maybe this time I hit the ground.

Maybe this time will be the last.

˜˜No one said it would be easy. The journey to healing is going to be long, painful and messy, but you know what else? Worth it. The journey is going to be worth it.˜˜

♦   ♦   ♦

Being awake is too hard.

Yet being asleep brings its pains as well.

You have to cope somehow, so you choose your poison, attempting to pick the lesser of evil.

No matter what you choose you just damage yourself a lot more, causing that much more pain in the long run.

Whether you pick up the bottle, the needle, or give a little slice, it takes it all away for moment .

A moment long enough to just breathe.

You try and focus on His face.

You try and not fall to your self-medicating ways.

You try with everything in you to fight off these feelings.

Drowning out your sorrows, drowning out your pain, you decide to pick your poison for the night so you can pretend to be alright.

♦   ♦   ♦

You are paralyzed and no one notices.

The world around you is moving fast but you are standing still.

Frozen.

No one seems to notice you. They are right in front of you but don't even glance your direction Too busy with their lives to notice that you are not okay.

♦   ♦   ♦

I am walking through this crowd but I have never felt so alone .

Won't somebody see past my imperfections.

Won't somebody take a minute to walk beside me.

Won't somebody take my hand and guide me.

The world keeps spinning but I am not moving.

I never wanted to be the fly on the wall.

But it seems that is what I have become.

In a world that won't slow down for anyone.

♦   ♦   ♦

Stuck in this past and can't get out.

♦   ♦   ♦

She turns on her computer and goes on her Netflix binge.

It turns off her brain; it drowns out the insides; it sends her to a different place forgetting all about reality.

It turns off her creativity; she puts her notepad away and stops her writing.

She stops her drawing; she stops her head; everything inside stops.

Drowning it all out with useless shows that seem to just absorb her time and take her away to someplace else.

♦   ♦   ♦

She will never open up.

She will never face the truth.

A closed book.

She has spent so much time erasing the pages and changing the stories that she is unsure of what is even real anymore.

The pain that she feels is real, yet she will never admit it's there.

"I feel no pain", she says so confidently you believe her.

A line she has rehearsed over and over again to get it right.

If only you could see what lies behind her lies.

If only she would tell you the truth.

If only she told you what really happened.

If only she told you the pain that she feels inside and the memories that haunt her.

Chilling her down to her bones.

They eat her up inside, tearing away with their claws and their teeth.

You will never see the truth.

You will never see the real pain she feels.

A little grimace that may cross her face is hardly even the tip of the mountains that lie underneath.

It's a wonder she is even here.

Maybe she thinks she deserves the tournament, so she lives another day.

All she thinks is that there are others who have had it worse.

Justifying in her mind that the pain she feels isn't real; that there are people who are in so much more pain. She feels so selfish and ashamed that she feels this pain. She is brave and mighty like a rock. She takes her punishment and will flash a grin afterwards to say that she is okay.

She will never open up.

She has closed her book and thrown away the key.

Every day she gets more and more tormented.

She remains strong.

Fighting.

Always fighting.

She looks at her painted skin to remind herself who she is.

She is relentless.

˜˜Never give up: keep on fighting. I know your pain. I know your insides. I see you. Stop saying you are okay. You are not. Stop dragging yourself into that pit. You deserve so much more. You CAN be okay. You won't have to lie. Just open your book, turn the pages and read it out loud. Find your voice through the pain. Come alive.˜˜

♦   ♦   ♦

Can you hear me? Is there someone there? Am I losing my mind? Am I all alone? Won't you rescue me?

7 Chasing the Darkness

Tried so hard to reach out but when I did it felt like no one could hear me.

◆   ◆   ◆

Feeling alone in a world full of people.

˜˜Searching ...looking for something ... some words to say to ease the hurting. Some action I can take to help it go away. I cannot hold you tonight but He can. Just ask: he is waiting.˜˜

◆   ◆   ◆

The memories, they keep flooding in.
A whiff of a flower sends me back to a whole different hour.
A breeze on my face sends me back to a whole different place.
I am there.
It's all real.
It's happening again.
How can this be?

Everything is colliding together. I become lost in time. Reality is a blur.
I forget where I am. I forget who I am.
These are not my hands, they are too old.
This is not my house, I have never seen it before.
This is not my body, it's far too heavy ... it's far too tall
... far too big.
I am just a young girl. I am lean. I am small.

I am in that place on that bed staring at the weave of the blanket with my imaginary friends: a very small family no bigger than two inches who go on adventures with their horse and dog.

I have been in the room for hours trapped on the bed, unable to move. Playing pictures in my head is the only thing keeping me from insanity. I hear outside children laughing and playing.

Screams of joy emit from them and fill the room with their sound.

The sun pours in from the window and beams down on my bed where my little imaginary family happily live.

My blanket covered in little Mickey Mouse. I imagine them all lighting up hot with joy and dancing along my bed.

But it's all in my head.

I am an adult.

I am a grown women.

I am so aged and gross.

My bones ache and my body is far too large .

I don't know how I got here.

I have a kid of my own who sleeps upstairs.

I crank the music to drown out the thoughts.

To drown out the years.

To drown out the memories.

I feel so gross.

I feel so old.

I look disgusting: my skin is flawed.

I have red dots on my face, holes and lines.

When did this happen? I am just a little girl.

Porcelain skin lightly freckled. Bleach blond hair that blows in the wind. A black lab whom I love so much.

Terrible parents who abuse me every chance they get.

It's all in my head.

Sometimes I am a young girl on the street. I am cold right down to my feet standing there beside the burnt building.

Smelling in the fumes of crime.

The fumes of pain and addiction.

Hearing the sound of sirens and screams in the night.

Seeing things that are such a frightful sight.

How did I get here? It's all in my head.

How did I get here? Shouldn't I be dead?

I am old and ragged. I can't stand the sight. I look in the mirror and I want to smash it. That is not me. Who am I??? I am not old; I am young. I am light on my feet and pale skinned. I am just a little girl.

Why am I so old so aged? How did I get like this? I can't take this disgusting body. I can't take this disgusting face.

I am just a child.

It's all in my head.

I should be dead.

♦ ♦ ♦

Sipping my whiskey to keep warm huddled up by the building what a frightful sight.

♦ ♦ ♦

Can you see them?

My inner demons who want nothing but the worst for me.

A battle. A never-ending battle.

An unanswered prayer to be free.

Can you see me?

♦ ♦ ♦

Peel back my skin, layer by layer.

I'm a caged animal trapped by my own skin.

Let me out.

Set me free.

Can't take the torment.

Can't take the pain.

Let me out.

Set me free.

Trapped inside of a body that's not mine.

I'm screaming. Can you hear me.

I'm screaming on the inside.

Let me out.

Set me free.

Can't take the torment.

Can't take the pain.

The Nightmare That Doesn't Let Go

It pulls you in. The screaming is so loud it rings in your ears. So vivid. So painful. It hurts.

Drugs flow through your veins. A mixture of anything that you could get your hands on. The poison rushes through your blood, reaching every crevice of your body. It helps calm you. Helps you to fight your way away from the screams that are buzzing in your head.

They are your screams. At least you think they are. Everything seems to be a blur. Your throat is burning. You feel pain all over.

"BEEP BEEP BEEP."

What is that sound?

This can't be real.

The screams seem to fade a bit as you try and focus on the beeping sound.

It's a dream. You're dreaming. Your alarm is trying to wake you for the day.

The screams still in your head, you find a way to a semi-conscious state. You must wake up. You must pull away from these screams and torture.

You move your hand around trying to find your alarm clock. You hit the snooze button.

The screams won't let you go. The pain won't let you go. You fight with all your might to pull away from the torture.

You can't.

You get sucked back in.

"LET ME GO!!!", you shout

You helplessly struggle to free yourself

You get so caught up in the torture, you forget. You forget about the beeping noise that reminded you that you were just dreaming. You're trapped.

You can't get out.

This is real.

Not a dream.

8 Cut

Take this pain
Slice me open
Make me bleed
Drain me dry
Let me die.

◆　◆　◆

Her blade is never quite sharp enough; she drags it across her skin slowly at first, but it hardly even leaves a mark, not even a single drop of blood.

A little more frantic this time, she digs in deeper and drags across harder, but it's the same thing; the same result: it's not enough.

Grabbing her knife sharpener, sharpening her tool impatiently.

When she feels like it's sharp enough she tries again.

It is a little better, but not enough, soon blood trickles along her arm.

It's not enough.

She wants to scream.

IT'S NOT ENOUGH.

DEEPER!!! I have to go deeper.

She is completely frantic now, grabbing kitchen knives in hopes that they will be sharper.

But nothing seems to be able to penetrate her skin deeply enough.

She drops the knives and collapses on the floor in a puddle.

"JUST LET ME GO," she yells into the sky.

"Just let me die."

"Please."

Begging and pleading to an invisible God she struggles to believe in, whilst blood smears onto the floor.

˜˜Not today. Put down that blade.˜˜

♦ ♦ ♦

Maybe if I just slice my skin.

Open it up and let it all out.

Let it pour out till the water is a deep red.

Maybe then this will all go away.

Maybe then I will feel better.

Like peeling the skin off an orange.

Open it up and see the fleshy insides.

How far down can I go?

How deep does this skin want to open up?

Maybe the deeper I dig the more will come out.

♦ ♦ ♦

I need to slice it away; slice my arms; slice my ribs and my legs. Oh man, open my flesh and let it out. I am so out of coping mechanisms. Been running mad trying to get this mind back on track to where it should be. I can't hold back anymore. I can't stop myself. This feeling is not going away. It's time to take it all away, have a bath until the water turns a deep red and not stop until I feel better.

˜˜There is a fire within you. Let it be the light that guides you.˜˜

♦ ♦ ♦

It can be anything, something so simple. You draw a red x on your hand to stand up for the injustice in the world. You post your picture with the hashtag #endIt. However, you find yourself staring at the picture of the x. Reminded of the time when slices of x's traveled along your arms and you had an x that was on your hand, much like the one now but one that stung and bled.

You glance at your arm but you hold your gaze for a little too long and find yourself mesmerized. You look at your scars that travel along the skin and are instantly drawn in. You accidentally scratch yourself on the corner of your door. It leaves a red line across your leg. This all leaves you with a craving: a craving to take a blade and touch it to your soft flesh. To feel a sting as you press a little harder. You slowly drag it across your flesh, leaving a fresh trail of open skin. You crave the feeling of the blade piercing through. The hot water that you pour over your bleeding wound seeps and pours down your arm: a deep red colour.

◆ ◆ ◆

She lays on the bathroom floor.

A drop of blood trickles down her arm and drops down on to the floor.

A blade is found snuggled between her thumb and index finger.

She hurts.

The pain is so hard to take. She should feel better. It should have worked.

All she wants is to go deeper to watch as her skin peels open.

To release her insides.

It's like the pain on the inside builds up so much that it needs a little help to get out.

Just slice a bit deeper.

Maybe if she forces herself to throw up it will go away.

Puke up everything that is inside of her. However, there is no food in her stomach.

It growls in protest, screaming out "please feed me." She can't. She can't eat. She can't sleep

All she can focus her energy on is to not take another, not take another slice.

Oh, it would have such a great release: grab a sharper tool of trade and slice her open.

In the midst of it, she lays there praying ... praying that God will take this away.

"Why? Why do I feel this way," she asks.

Her insides are screaming, trying to claw their way out, yet she can barely get her voice above a whisper.

She tries to force out a voice but no sound comes out.

A meek little whispe.r

She momentarily sets down her little blade to clutch her side.

She curls up tight and winces because it hurts, oh man it hurts so bad.

Her face distorts as though she is in excruciating pain ... because she is!

She is fighting.

Everything inside of her just wants more.

Everything is screaming on the inside and it hurts so much.

She is so nauseous and just wants to hurl, get everything out.

She rolls over in pain; it's sheer torment.

How long can she fight this?

She tries to write out her emotions, yet it doesn't seem to help.

She needs this.

She needs to go deeper.

To release a little more.

Just one more.

One deep opening to release this pain,

She picks up her blade again.

~ ~ *This is not what you were meant for.*
   You have to be stronger than your urges. ~ ~

◆   ◆   ◆

She places the cool blade down on the counter and traces her finger gracefully along her wrist. Pausing for a moment to just take a breath, the trigger is too much for her. She reaches down and fumbles with the toilet paper frantically trying to tear it off the roll. "Just one, just one" she repeats the words in her head like she is trying to memorize lines in a play. Words she has told herself time and time again, yet never followed through.

She sets down the wadded up toilet paper and in the same motion picks up the little blade. She touches the blade just above her thumb knuckle, presses down lightly and carefully slides it across her skin. So lightly the skin hardly breaks. A mere paper cut that does not even bleed. Just enough pressure and stamina to test the sharpness of the blade; not to break through too many skin layers.

Satisfied with the results of her tool she brings it to her forearm. "Just one," she quietly mumbles under her breath.

She takes the sharp side of the blade and presses down into her skin. Slowly she drags the blade across about a centimetre, applying steady pressure. Her skin peels open like a book. She watches her skin. When it first opens, it is white inside. After what seems like a few seconds - but is merely half a second - little beads of red start seeping out of the opening, slowly at first, then the whole line becomes covered in red until the blood starts trickling down her arm.

She grabs her toilet paper and presses it against her wound the white toilet paper absorbs the dark liquid like they were meant to be together. She lifts up the paper to peer at her cut. It is still seeping blood and now she had little bits of tissue dust stuck to the surrounding area of her fresh wound. Without further thought the blade is back in her hand and already pressed two millimetres away from her still-bleeding cut. She presses down and drags the blade across her arm just like the other one, keeping her gaze directly on her skin the entire time. Waiting to feel the pain; the satisfactory ... nothing! This cut hardly nicked the surface. Little beads of blood pushed through and then stopped. Without thinking she frantically tries again, and again, and again, and again. Each time she drags the blade across her skin she released a little bit more emotional build-up, she feels a little bit more relief. Once she notices how far up her cuts are getting, she quickly grabs the tissues and presses it on her arm.

Relief. She feels like she can breathe again. The toilet paper once white, is now a deep red with only white tips. "No, no, no!" She exhales with a bit of panic, her forearm now covered with two inches of neat little lines, each line bleeding at its own pace; some dripping some hardly bleeding. Thoughts go through her mind: "can't I just erase this? What have I done? How will I cover this? No one can know! Why can't these be erasable?!?!"

Instantly she regrets her decision.

˜˜*You have to keep on going. The world needs you.* ˜˜

♦   ♦   ♦

Feel the world crushing you.

Your time is due.

Now stop feeling so blue.

Pick up the blade.

Look at what you made.

They will fade.

This isn't a game,

slice the pain,

miss a vein.

Maybe there is another way.

But not today.

Now are you feeling okay?

Put down the letter,

put on a sweater.

are you feeling better?

9 SUICIDE

Drowning In Plain Sight

Some days I come close.

Some days I can see it

The end, the end is so close I can taste it on my lips.

I can see it on the faces of my friends as they get the news. I can hear it: it's the silence at the end of a movie as the screen goes dark after the ending scene, except the credits don't roll and there is no sequel.

It leaves you sitting there wondering "that's it?? It's over?"

I can feel it.

It wraps around me with its slithering arms, then pulls me in.

I can feel myself sinking.

I feel it burn into my lungs as the water pools in and the air is pushed out.

I can see around me all my friends standing around as though I am in a glass box.

At first they open the door and come in but then they get busy.

I watch them as they carry on with themselves. I tap on the glass wondering if they can see me. Sometimes they throw a glance my way and mouth, "in a minute", but what they don't seem to notice is the water is starting to fill up. It starts at my toes and then makes its way up my legs.

I knock on the glass: they don't hear me.

I bang.

They don't hear me.

The water is rising.

I watch them as it engulfs me.

They laugh over their coffee. They are busy talking to their children. They are all there as I drown and breathe my last breath. They are oblivious to what has happened.

˜˜This is not your way out. It's your time to rise not lay down. ˜˜

A Father's Love

She was so close to ending it all.

She looked up to the sky and said "f#ck it all."

It's time to take the leap.

It's time to fall.

But somehow she stood tall.

She took the jump.

Yet as she fell there was no end.

There was no landing and then darkness.

His wings.

His wings carefully embraced her as she was falling.

He took the fall for her.

Wrapped in the safety of his wings he protected her.

His beautiful and perfect face stained from tears.

So many times he would watch in pain as she would destroy herself just a little more: a self-hate so strong she would slice herself open repeatedly, never quite deep enough. The word "fat" permanently scarred into her body.

He wept.

He held her as close as He could and yet she was so consumed by the darkness she could not feel His embrace.

He would shout at her, "YOU ARE MAKING ME CRY, YOU ARE HURTING ME." But she would only pause for a moment then continue her path of self-destruction.

A path that led her to the end.

A path that led her to take the plunge. To end it.

Of course, He saved her. He always has: every single time. He grabs her before she falls and carries her. He is always there right by her side protecting her from death at the hand of others, but even more so protecting her from her biggest enemy,

Herself.

Safe in His embrace.

Safe in her Father's wings.

◆　◆　◆

The only sound to be heard is laboured breathing: the jingle of dog tags and their steps as they run.

The cars are covered in a sparkly frost and the glitter under the streetlights.

Her breath comes out in clouds as she exhales

Her fingers are completely frozen. She cannot even close them enough to grasp her dog's leash. He runs in perfect stride beside her, not faltering a single step. If her legs start to buckle or she has an overwhelming dizzy spell, he moves his body in front of her legs to stop her from running, and so that she can lean into him and support her body onto his sturdy shoulders. He waits there with his body positioned to hold her until he gets a satisfactory pat and a "good boy let's go".

Then he falls back in line at her side, so close his fur rubs against her cold legs.

Traffic is sparse and she travels to a main road. Exiting the sidewalk, she veers onto the road as her dog attempts to guide her back onto the sidewalk by gently pushing himself against her, toward the pathway, worried that they are walking a dangerous path. After a correction, he falls in line again and releases the pressure on her side.

There are headlights in the distance. They are traveling at a fair speed. She is now directly in the middle of its path. She runs as fast as she can directly towards the headlights. The lights are getting closer and coming faster. They probably can't see her: it's not a well-lit road. It would be quick. It would be painful. It would be freedom.

Mesmerized by the lights she stops, feels the air with her frozen hand and touches it as if feeling it for the last time while saying goodbye. She listens. It's so silent outside. It's like the world is on pause. You can almost hear the cold night air: it has a different sound to it. Empty; it sounds empty.

Gazing upwards she sees stars.

Wow. They are beautiful. A black night with tiny white dots sprinkled among the canvas. You can even see the dipper clear as can be, twinkling away.

She closes her eyes to take it all in, inhaling deeply. Even with her eyes closed, she can see the twinkling stars.

Twinkle...

Twinkle twinkle little star.

How I wonder...

An imagine flashes through her mind, An image of a small child sleeping in her arms while she sings her nightly song to him.

"What you are, up above the world so high"

He nestles into her arms so perfectly she can almost hear his laugh as she tickles him and he squeaks and squirms.

Flashing her eyes open to see his beautiful face she looks at the headlights still speeding toward her like time resumed.

She dashes off the road and jumps back onto the grass.

The car speeds on by as though nothing happened. Because it didn't.

Just a thought. Just a dream. Maybe a hope. Maybe a wish.

Saved again by a beautiful little face. A little face that will always be there to help her fight through those hard times.

♦ ♦ ♦

Oh, how the world would be a better place without your hideous face.
Oh, how glorious it would be if you took away your life.
It would end all of this trife.
You know the way out you hold it in your hand.
Stop trying to bury your head in the sand.
This is the only way out.
Don't even pout.
You know I am right.
The answer is in plain sight.
Stop trying to fight the inevitable and take your life away
Oh, how you have gone astray
It's time for you to end
Not time to mend.

˜˜*It's all a lie. Don't fall into this death trap. I wish you could see. I wish you could see the plans I have for your life. I wish that you could see how much I love you.*˜˜

♦ ♦ ♦

Jump.
Jump.
The words scream out inside your head.
You play it over and over in your mind.
You imagine your body falling.
Falling.

You watch as it makes contact with the ground.

You picture the different ways you land.

Some nice and neat, others end with a mess that can never fully be cleaned.

You imagine your friends as they get the news: "I didn't even know she was sad" they say in disbelief. "She seemed okay."

You imagine your son as he grows up without you. He holds so much hate toward you. "She didn't even love me; she was a coward who chose to be selfish and abandon me."

You just hope that he would understand: understand that if it was not for him, you would have been gone so much sooner. Understand that you fought long and hard just for him. That all you ever wanted was for him to have the perfect life. To grow up better than you did.

All you would hope for is that the world would see: would see that a smile or a laugh could be so deceiving, see that not everything is as it seems.

You have cried out for help so many times and yet everyone thought you were bluffing but what they didn't know was that each time they responded to your cries they would help you see a hope that wasn't there before, however the ringing line on the other end was a sound you heard too often that old faithful answering machine a sound you seemed to be a little familiar with and so you would struggle on your own.

Grabbing your sword and armour you fight your battle alone.

Every.

Single.

Night.

Fighting.

Not today: this fight is done.

Jump. Take the plunge.

Dive down into death.

Oh, it's so close she can taste it.

Freedom.

˜˜It gets easier. It really does.˜˜

◆ ◆ ◆

She lays in the tub, the water is painted red from her fresh wounds.

Her body is stinging.

She inhales deeply and lays back into the tub until her head is fully submerged.

She holds her breath.

The sound of her heartbeat fills her ears from beneath the water, echoing against the tub walls.

The heartbeat that she wants to stop.

The heartbeat she is always plotting against.

A way out is all she can think of. Planning a way out, she thinks of her options, and a small bubble escapes her lips. Another bubble follows and she tries to force herself to hold on just a little longer. She focuses on the sound of her heartbeat and imagines the silence. The sound of it beating its very last beat: she can almost hear it in her head already.

Opening her eyes under the water she catches a glimpse of something red above the water, and she remembers. Bursting out of the blood-soaked water, she gasps for air and pants heavily as she tries to regain her breath. She lets out a cough and looks on the edge of the tub at the red container:

Spider man shampoo.

The reason she is still here.

The reason she holds on.

The reason she still fights.

The reason her heart still beats.

Her son.

It's all she has to hold on to.

It's the one thing in her life that keeps her holding on.

The one thing in her life that can stop her from ending it all.

The only thing she has to live for.

His smile, his face, his bright eyes.

He keeps her alive.

◆ ◆ ◆

Beads of sweat run along your flesh.

Hairs standing up tall on your arms.

A shiver, a pant of heat.

You did it.

You took the final plunge.

You will finally be free.

Your head is pounding and everything around you keeps turning black.

It is like someone keeps dimming the lights in the room

You let it in.

Don't fight the darkness.

A sigh of relief emits from your lungs.

It's over.

You are free.

You close your eyes for the final time and let the darkness cover you.

˜˜Fight. Fight. Fight.˜˜

Not now, not like this. This is not how you leave. It's not your time. It's not your place. Open your eyes; search for a light in the darkness. Stay awake, don't fade. Pull yourself up, breathe in and breathe out, concentrate on something to keep yourself awake...

Fading...

Fading...

NO. FIGHT. Not yet, not now, it's not the day. Get yourself together. This is not the way. It is not too late: this is not your fate. Fight. Use all your might.

Do not die.

It's not time for goodbye.

♦ ♦ ♦

I sit here pondering, needle glistening in my hand.

There is a way to end this all.

There is a way to be free.

Fill up the plunger and take the plunge. Fall deep into the darkness to never return. Let the fluid rush through my body burning and tearing as is goes.

It will reach my shattered heart and touch every broken piece, turning it blackl Then it will crumble to dust.

I will be free.

˜˜*You have come too far to give up now.*˜˜

10 Fragments

At least if it's sleepless, it's dreamless.

Toss and turn.

Back and forth.

Maybe some whiskey will help.

Toss in some sleeping pills: that should do the trick.

Cravings, cravings so strong they make you rock back and forth.

So strong you can't close your eyes.

What's keeping you awake tonight?

Is it the cravings?

Maybe it's the memories.

Maybe it's the calories.

Maybe it's everything.

Drink a little, cut a little, drink a little, cut a little, repeat.

Drown it out with blood and whiskey.

Daddy's girl

I thought I smelled you today. I stopped dead in my tracks when the scent touched my nose. I know it wasn't you, but it was so similar. I miss you. I wish it didn't have to be this way for us. You were everything to me.

I was just a little girl. You were the only one I called Daddy.

The only Dad I ever had. Oh, how it pains me to say that word: "daddy," "dad." A lump in my throat can be felt the moment I utter the word. Even writing it causes the lump to grow. I stood in the middle of the road frozen in my tracks, my own little boy clutching my hand and singing a song. Rambling on about nothing and yet everything My dog nudging my hand, wondering why we suddenly stopped.

We did this once.

You and I.

I don't ever remember holding your hand, but I remember talking away about nothing to you as we walked the dog. I was just like my son is: I didn't stop talking. You would probably just zone me out.

But man, did I ever look up to you. I wanted you to notice me. Notice that I, too, could sand down drywall and be a builder just like you. I would grow up and be you. I would fix those big ol' trucks, redo a basement, build a fence: anything you could do I would do. It's possible you never loved me the way I loved you. I craved your attention. I wanted a Daddy. I wanted nothing more than to be your little girl. Just a little Daddy's girl, but you didn't notice me.

You didn't notice how I would try and please you, grabbing scraps of wood and nails, trying to create a masterpiece to impress you. You wanted a tomboy and that is what I became.

You used to call me "Squirt" and "Kiddo." I loved it. It was a pet name that only you called me.

It's funny how often I think of you. Every day I wish it could have been different. Maybe if you were my biological father. Maybe if your wife was not so crazy. Maybe if you just could have seen the potential I had: my drive to please you, maybe then I would have been worth fighting for. Maybe you would have put down the bottle and stood up to your wife while she abused us ... and said "ENOUGH!"

I know you tried. I remember the yelling: "You are too hard on the girls", but you let her win. You let her control you, as she did everyone. I would not have survived if it was not for you. You see, when you were away at work, the abuse was that much worse. The sound of your blue Ford Ranger is a sound I will never forget: the whine of that engine, I still hear clear as day. The smell of your aftershave as you sat and read the newspaper with your morning coffee. I wish you'd have looked up. I wish you'd have seen me for who I was. I wish you'd have known the excitement that ran through me when I saw your truck in the driveway because you were home early. I literally could feel my heart jump, because it meant that I did not have to be left alone with her. I wish you had known much pain I would feel about losing you. I wish you had known that I didn't run away from you: I ran away from her.

I didn't try to kill myself because of you. It was because of her.

I wish you had known how much I looked up to you. That day you told me that I should just die, and you threw the bottle of pills at me because you were so fed up with me: I wish you had known that it wasn't you. It wasn't you from whom I was broken. It wasn't your fault.

It was her.

I will always be a Daddy's girl.

♦   ♦   ♦

I'm a lion.

I prowl.

I work.

I stalk.

Irresistible.

Always catch my prey.

This is me.

˜˜*There is a reason you are here. Maybe you are looking at this page in search of hope, looking for a sign, a reason why. Maybe you are looking in all the wrong places. Don't look in the box, look on the outside.*˜˜

◆ ◆ ◆

Stuck on the streets.

Can't get free.

Abusive relationship.

Can't get free.

Exploitation.

Can't get free.

Suicidal inside a body that refuses to die.

Can't get free.

Show up at church; worship with the King I have rejected time and time again.

Hurt and damaged beyond repair.

The pain is unbearable, the war inside never ending.

Can't get free.

˜˜*I see you. I hear you. You are not alone.* ˜˜

Halloween sadness

Just another Halloween sitting in the dark so the children to do not come to the door.

Peering through the half-open curtains, watching the children run and play. Tears roll down your face as you watch them eagerly running door to door, dragging their parents behind them. Some tall children, some small children who have yet to take their first steps - all bundled up in their costumes, clutching a little basket full of candy they can't even eat yet... spilling it as they go. More tears rolling down your face; full of too many emotions for one person. Sadness, anger, regret, loneliness, longing, a broken heart.

That should be you. Chasing your toddler down the street trying to keep them on the sidewalk. Keeping them from tripping on people's steps in a costume that is way too baggy and dragging on the ground as they run along. Maybe you carry them back home snuggled in your arms, quietly slip off their shoes and tuck them in costume and all. Maybe you bring them home and they are bouncing off the walls from a sugar high, or throwing a fit because they really want to eat that sketchy looking half-wrapped candy. Whatever it is, that is what you are supposed to be doing right now, but instead you look on with your shattered heart; longing toward the children who are dressed in all sort of costumes and attire.

Thinking of your own child whom you have lost.

◆   ◆   ◆

The light of her smile.

The mystery in her gaze.

The love for her child.

The waves in her hair.

The paint on her nails.

The giggle escaping her lips.

A light shrug of her shoulders.

A sigh of relief .

A tear rolling down her face landing in the hand of her Saviour.

He catches her tears and wipes her cheeks.

Whispering in her ear.

"Rest my Child, I am here.

It's going to be okay.

I love you."

˜˜Excuse me? Yeah you, YOU are worth it.˜˜

Forced to walk away

Just a baby, eight months old. Looks up into his Mother's eyes and giggles as she tickles him. He senses something is wrong. Her eyes are red and she seems off. He tries cheering her up with his smiles and giggles. She places him in the crib, kisses his head and walks away with tears building in her eyes, waiting to fall.

He screams. Can you see his pain?

It's clear as day written on his face.

He is so young he can't hide his emotions.

He clutches the crib bars with all his might, while crying a heart-stopping cry, hoping that she will turn around and come back.

She doesn't.

Where did his Mommy go?

◆ ◆ ◆

She doesn't want to go to sleep tonight.

She's afraid that the demons will take her away.

11 A LETTER TO MY CHILD
AND THOSE I LOVE

I am scared. You see I love you. I know it might not seem like it all the time. I push, I pull, I run away, but I am just terrified. I am fighting every day to stay here. Everyday is a battle for me and I choose life day after day, but you see as the sun goes down and it's quiet, the darkness seems to engulf me. It wraps me up so tight it chokes me. I do my best to fight it off. I think of you guys, I picture my child's face, I picture your faces. I imagine your sadness and anger as you get the news that I did not make it, that I was a coward, I laid down my swords and shields and I let the darkness take me away.

I love you. In my darkest moments my only thought is ending it. Sometimes those thoughts are so strong that I take action and that is scary for me. I don't want to leave you. I don't want to go. I want to stay here with you.

I have gone over my last moments in my mind so many times and it hurts to know the pain you would feel. So every day I pick up my swords and I fight. I am fighting for you. I am holding on for you. So I can only hope that you will hold onto me in return. That you will understand the battle I am in and hold me close. Please don't let me go.

This is not a goodbye; however, it has to be said in case it gets to the end.

In case I lose this fight.

I love you. If I let go, it is time for you to let go as well. My fight is over now: the battle is done. You helped me get this far. Thanks to you I made it as far as I did. No phone call, no text or visit could have prevented this, so don't you dare feel guilty because that is NOT on you.

But I will stay, I choose to remain here and fight. I choose to stay, for when I look into my child's eyes I see a future. I see love. When I am with you guys I laugh so hard my face hurts. You give me the strength to continue.

I will pick up my battle ax and slay my demons night after night, for you. If I cannot do it for myself I will do it for you.

For those of you also on a struggle right now I am asking you: please pick up your battle ax and fight with me. You are not alone. We will stand tall and fight this battle together. Please do not let go, there is an entire world out there waiting for you. An unknown crowd in the background cheering you on.

I am rooting for you.

You are not in this alone. Together we stand strong.

My story is not over and neither is yours.

THE BEGINNING.

12 LIGHT!

I had a very bad night, I was so overwhelmed by my life all I wanted was for it to end but not in the way I normally do. Normally, when I want my life to end, I want to end it in suicide. But I had this complete moment of despair. I could see my future life. I could see my freedom but when I looked in front of me, all I see are my old ugly cracked floors, the reflection of police lights in my house and the dark gloom that I currently am living in.

I am not one to show emotion. I often shove everything down and if I feel those tears start to build I swallow them with anything I can so they won't start. I spent at least three hours listening to worship songs and bawling. This is big for me to admit because I hate people knowing if I cry.

I told God that I was done. I was done living life the way I was. I was done living on the bottom and living with this pain, shackled in chains like a dog on a leash. I have always seen myself as a bird in a cage, a tiger in a zoo, I am very free-spirited and yet I have been trapped in this cage.

Song after song came like words directly from God's mouth. Just as I would start to think my crying was over, another song would start and I would cry again. I cannot describe my emotions: I am not sure if I was sad, mad or whatever. I just know that in that moment, I couldn't take it anymore. Often if I feel emotion, I drink, cut, do drugs or turn some non-Christian music up loud and dance it away. This time, I wasn't craving any of that. I guess maybe I needed the release instead of fighting it off. I needed to accept my feelings, lay down my sword and my shield and surrender. I chose to surrender everything including my fight. I have been fighting this darkness for years but I never really bring God into it because I think, "I can handle it in my own; I don't need anyone to fight my battles for me."

I needed to let go.

I begged God for freedom; I begged for a new life for hours, from daylight into the dark night. I didn't know one could cry so many tears.

I don't remember going to sleep that night, but I eventually curled up with my worship music, completely exhausted.

When I woke up, and ever since then, I have felt this hope, this fire, this burning in me to seek more. It feels strange for me to say but I actually believe I feel happy. I don't remember ever feeling like this before. It's really strange but I feel as though the fire has been lit within me. I don't want it to die. I have spent every single day of my entire life wishing I would die, praying that God would end me and take me home. It's been an eternity of torment under the spirit of death. This is the beginning, this is the start of my revival.

I laid it down; I laid it all down. I'm letting go of my "strength" and letting God show me his has taken me years. I'm surrendering this battle and letting him fight it for me. That's a miracle in itself.

I feel like it's not over. I honestly am scared of this next phase, mostly because I'm afraid of messing it up. But I refuse to let fear win. But I can see the chains falling, and not only from me. I can see the chains falling off everyone. I can see a world of freedom. I can see myself up on that stage spreading hope and telling my story. I can see my life, and it is good. As God said when he made the world, "It is good," he says that as he makes me whole and makes me new. Through these battles I am holding on, holding onto my Father. I am letting God fight them for me as hard as they might be.

This is HIS life. He is making me new.

I can see my freedom, I can see your freedom!

It's coming!

◆   ◆   ◆

The light of her smile.
The mystery in her gaze.
The love for her child.
The waves in her hair.
The paint on her nails.
The giggle escaping her lips.
A light shrug of her shoulders.
A sigh of relief.
A tear rolling down her face landing in the hand of her Saviour.
He catches her tears and wipes her cheeks,
Whispering in her ear,
"Rest my Child, I am here.
It's going to be okay.
I love you."

◆   ◆   ◆

Today I see a man looking over the edge of a bridge with police cars on either side of him.
To this man, I want to say,
"I have been there; I know that it hurts right now."

You look over the edge and it all plays through your head; you time it out in your mind and the cars become mesmerizing as they zoom beneath you.

You can see it, you can see it all, you picture yourself as you take the final leap, a leap to end your life. Please listen to me. You don't want your life to end. You just want your pain to end; you just want the circumstances to end. There is a world out there waiting for you. A world out there that is begging you to stay.

You may feel alone, like everyone is against you, but trust me when I say you are not alone. We stand together, all of us who have felt those feelings. We have looked death in the eyes and said no.

You can too.

Say, No!

Your life is far more valuable than you know.

It's tempting, I know. It is so easy to just take that step off the edge, spread your arms and salute the world goodbye. You are a fighter. It takes courage, it takes strength to take that step down and say "No, no I will not go, I will stay."

So I know you will never see this dear sir, but I ask of you, if it is not too late, please step back. Say "No" with me. Stand with me and turn away from the eyes and the grasp of death, I wish you could see how worthy you truly are.

EPILOGUE

First off, you must know that I am okay. Every single year has gotten easier. Challenges are there, yes, but you know what else is there? A freedom, a light that was not there before. I am on the journey to healing, I am on the pathway to a better life. You can be too. I know it is not easy; I know you just want to give up, but you have to hang on okay? There is a light and it's calling you. Your chains are going to fall off and you will be set free. I can see it, I can see your freedom and it is beautiful. Just wait and see what is out there for you.

Maybe this is far from your story. This isn't my entire story: there is still lots left to be said, but maybe I will save that for my next book. There are people out there today, right now, this very second, who are being used. They are being abused in ways you never thought imaginable: horror stories far more gruesome than mine. My heart breaks for them and all I want is their freedom. My hope in writing this book is to bring hope to those who don't feel any, and to cut off any feelings of loneliness people have, because those feelings are fatal. Those are the ones that sneak in and hurt the most, but they are a lie. I have to remind myself of that often: I am not alone.

I also hope to bring awareness to the struggle that so many out there are facing today, be it abuse, addiction, slavery, and/or mental health. The things I have written have painted a fairly clear picture; however, it is not perfectly clear. Often these things are hidden. You may not even realize what is going on right next door to you. Many times in my life no one could see what was really going on. Professionals missed it; doctors, social workers. It's like I was screaming out, "Help me," to no one. I would do everything I could for someone to see just a little bit of my reality, but nobody came to help me. No one came. There are many points in my life where something could have been done differently; where if just one person had stepped in and said "enough", then maybe things would be different for me today. Maybe I would not have had to go through what I did. However, then maybe you would not be reading this. You can no longer say you didn't know. You are no longer blind to the problems people are facing every single day, whether it be abuse, mental health or addiction. So I would like to ask you something. I would like you to be the one who steps up: the one who says "enough," if you see or suspect an injustice. Don't you dare turn your head. Stand up! Use your voice for the voiceless and say "STOP". You have no idea what an impact you can make on the world if you can simply be brave enough to stand up and say "enough is enough!".

Let's put an end to this.

Together.

84187839R00053